A LEGION OF DRUMS

AN ANTHOLOGY OF POEMS

A LEGION OF DRUMS

AN ANTHOLOGY OF POEMS

K I LAIBUTA

Published By
Bridgehouse Limited
PO Box 6455-00300, Nairobi
Website: www.bridgehouseconsultants.net

A LEGION OF DRUMS
AN ANTHOLOGY OF POEMS

Copyright ©Dr. K I Laibuta 2020

No part of this book may be reproduced or utilized in any form or by any means, electronic or mechanical, including photocopying, recording, or by any information storage or retrieval systems, without permission in writing from the publisher or copyright holder. Any unauthorised reproduction of this work shall constitute a copyright infringement and render the doer liable under both civil and criminal law.

Cover Design and Layout by Senzafine Limited
www.senzafine.co.ke

ISBN: 978-9914-702-46-0

Dedication

To my granddaughter Nina, and to every child to whom much is owed to the ends of joy and comfort, and to freedom and peace.

Foreword

Piecing together this collection of poems has been an exciting journey worth the decades of reflection, dreams and lamentations that characterize the voices that echo in the reader's mind, much like a thousand drums whose incessant rumble urges us on without letup.

The pieces comprise a record of moments of right and wrong, love and hate, joy and gloom, cheer and distress. The book is a collection of tales told in subdued voices of faceless multitudes who run the race for life in a dark world over which neither master nor slave can gain mastery. It visualizes a journey in the turbulent world of visions and dreams, war and peace, trust and betrayal, hope and courage. The collection mirrors the taste of bitter and sweet with which we contend in our strife and grueling race for life before our dreams come true to usher in a bright new world of freedom and peace.

Contents

Across the Bridge 1
A Day with Rosa 3
A Flight in Hope 4
A Friend in Deed 5
A Legion of Drums 7
All Alone 9
Alone 11
A Race In The Dark 13
Before I Go Away 15
Counting Time 17
Dancing in the Rain 19
Daring to Dream 21
Demons at Play 22
Do Let Me Be 24
Eye of the Storm 26
Faces of Development 28
Flowers that Wouldn't Bloom 29
Forgotten Dreams 31
Give Me Time 33
Here Comes Democracy 35
If Only 37
If Only I Could Have My Way 38
If Only It Would Rain 40
In Angel's Arms 42
In Awe of Gods They Do Not Know 44
In Memoriam 46

In Praise of Angels of My Day 48
In Solitude 50
In the Eye of the Storm 51
In the Name of Democracy 53
In the Name of Love 55
In War and Peace 57
Let There Be Light 59
Lost in Your World 61
Love long Gained 62
Love's Hiding Place 64
My Turn at Play 66
Prosperity 67
Season's End 68
Talking to Me 70
Tell Me Tales 72
Tell Them! 74
The Aftermath 76
The Bitter Fruitage of Their Reign 78
The Cockroach Dance 80
The Cost of Love? 81
The Day You Went Away 83
The Earth Will Sing 84
The Lunacy of Love 86
The Price of Peace 87
The Sunset of Our Day 88
The Vanity of Love 90
The Vanity of Man 91
The Winds of Change 93

The Wind Storm in Conspiracy 95
To Love and Hate 98
To Those that You Shall Say Goodbye 99
Vessels of Broken Dreams 100
Waiting for Grass to Grow 101
Waiting For You 103
Wars Without End 105
Wartime Dreams 107
Watching the World 109
What Would I See 111
When I Am Gone 113
When I grow Old 114
When Life Began 116
When Mama Starts to Pray 118
When Papa Cries 120
When the Rain is Gone 122
When Will Day Break 124
Where is Love Laid? 126
Where is the Fire? 127
Where Will We Go? 129
Whirling With the Wind 131
Who Am I? 133
Who will You mourn? 135
Would God Send Us Rain? 137
You Sing No More 140
You Will Be Borne Again 142

Across the Bridge

The visions stirred in racing minds,
The pacing dreams in youthful zest,
Have this far come on pilgrimage
To lay petitions at the feet
Of those enthroned on wickedness
From which they harvest bounteously
And reap the fruits of lawlessness
By which the demons have held sway.

"Give us some bread," their plaintiff cry
Has rang for decades in loud wails
That bounce in echoes through the lands
On which the sun would not bow down
Until a record of their pleas
On sacred altar has been laid
And peoples gathered in resolve
To find rebirth across the bridge.

What then will become of these kings
When those dark clouds in all their might
Come pelting them with blinding blows

And dash them into smithereens
To let new heavens and new earth
Give forth new sprouts when Kingdom comes
To lead the righteous and the meek
To healing springs across the bridge?

A Day with Rosa

My Rosa's day in length and breadth
Is Mama's journey of lifetimes
Through which she peers beyond bare clouds
To share a smile with some sun rays
In hope that darkness at nightfall
Would bring her joy despite her toils
To set her table with no means
That man and son may her bread break
In prayerful thanks day after day
That would give way to nights of gloom
When Rosa's heart would seek repose
In shelters of his yawning arms.

It is this man whose love was known
To Rosa from her youthful age
When hearts in strange ways closed their ranks
As devilish charms took centre stage
On theatres of their warm embrace
In which the poor and rich alike
Exchange their vows in gratitude
For love's ways that knows no retreat
When lovers lost in fantacies
Take refuge in compounded dreams.

A Flight in Hope

This life, like a chilling snarling wind,
Bears my weary wings from here to there
While all I can is flap and flop
As stormy rains come beating down
To tell me tales of known defeats
All moments when I raise my eyes
To catch the light of morning sun
And bid farewell to mournful gloom
Of those dark nights that trailed me close
Despite my plea to let me go.

Where shall I go in fright and flight
While mounds and hills my paths blockade
From East to West, from North to South,
Whose winds in their conspiracy
Join hands to blow and wash ashore
The dreams that I had once espoused
Of life of pleasures and of joy
That lie in caskets and in tombs
Engraved with hope on epitaphs
That chance had lettered in fine gold.

A Friend in Deed

Who but true friend would your woes share
And lighten burdens that you bear
Despite sorrows you persevere
As on your own you fret in fear
Before true friends do soon appear
To dust your feet without a sneer
In times when foes that jeer and cheer
Would blur the visions you hold dear?

Who but true friend would barriers tear
And bring down fences built in tiers
That classify societies
In friends and foes, that have or want;
In colours of mere countenance
As though the stranger you behold,
The one whose lineage you disclaim,
Descends from forms unknown to gods
While you and I were civilized
In realms beyond humanity?

Who but a friend in truth indeed,
With smothered hearts would comfort share
For no returns or prize to gain
But Self-effacing gallantry
With which true friends in honesty
Come forth with kisses to betray
Unbounded love without pretext
Or treacheries that plague our foes.

A Legion of Drums

Before God sends us rain again,
A widow wails on muted tombs
As orphans hold their empty bowls
While kings and princes in their robes
Stride back and forth in prideful gait
In banquet halls and ballroom floors
To celebrate some season's end
With vintage wines and sumptuousness
As milling crowds in wanton haste
Search clods of earth for fallen grain.

The village stirs in its disease
Then clears its throat in sad refrain
Amid its murmurs in revolt
As drumbeats roll to trumpet calls
That all might rise at palace gates
To bring an end to royal feasts
While crowds in hunger and in thirst
Have lost all hope for brighter days
Until God's kingdom comes in haste
And gives us rain to grow our grain.

A LEGION OF DRUMS

Let trumpets call and drumbeats roll
In legions most unknown to man
To herald season of new days
When kings and princes of this day
Will sure like hounds have had their day
Before their starlight fades away
And suns that rose in their gone days
Will leave no trace of night or day
As multitudes rise on the day
When tears and sorrows go their way.

All Alone

The moment since you went away
The crowds of trees as though to mourn
Shed all their leaves in sympathy
As muted birds that had once sang
Would not in whisper or in song
Tell tales of days when you and I
Had strolled these fields clang hand in hand
Before your flight to distant lands
Six thousand miles beyond the seas
Where there would be no bed for two
Or bodies locked in warm embrace
Except in dreams or memories
In which we bathe night after day
As dawn and sunset ceaseless race
Chasing the next after the last
For countless days and lonesome nights
When all I have for an embrace
Is the only one I learned to be.

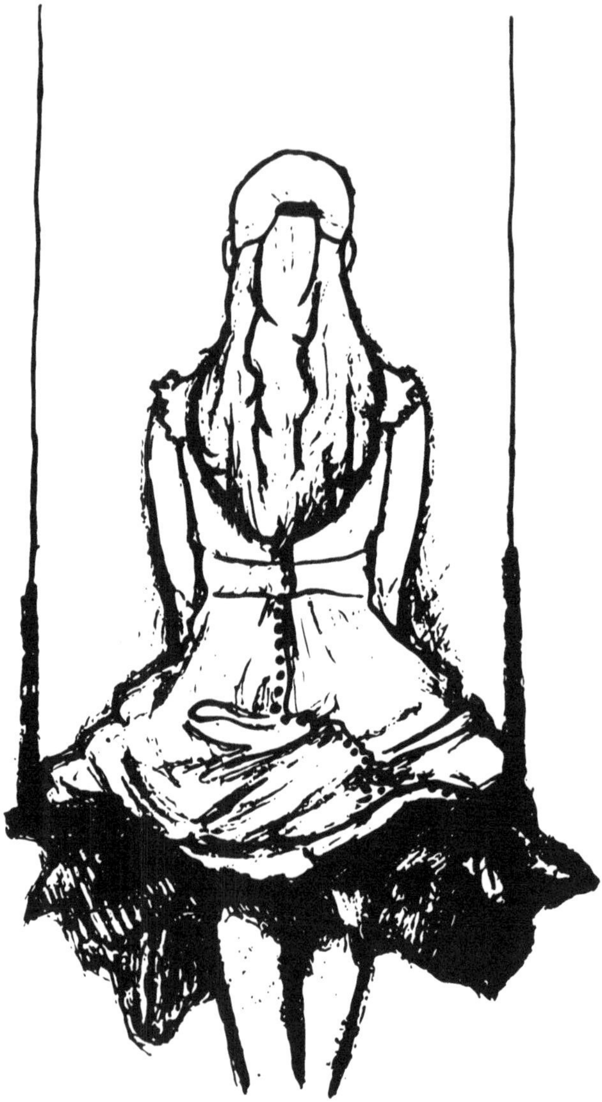

Alone

In sluggish hours of muted nights
When sun and moon their face conceal
From lonesome stars in tombs then laid
He tossed and stirred in crumbling dreams
While dawn had been on pilgrimage
To distant realms beyond the seas
On which he sails in fleeting thoughts
That life's fruits borne to lifelessness
Embraced by souls with whom he played
Would cure the plague of lonesomeness.

This divan on which he was laid
The moment that she had been wed
To one unknown to love's delight
For reasons that none would have known
Has crumbled much like all their dreams
With nothing left to consummate
A marriage one would celebrate
With eagerness to kiss the bride.

Alone, the groom in solitude
Has ink on nibs upon a scroll
To tell tales that none could have told
In spoken words without restraint
As night and day in one accord
Would, in the arms of ticking time,
Count seasons when he, all alone,
Would bear the burdens of one's mind
On scripts on which love's tales were told
Of treacherous lovers of his day.

A Race In The Dark

When lifeless trees had their leaf shed
And berries on so barren earth lay
To join the rot of nuts and figs
Unfeeling storms from distant seas,
To docks and lands the boatmen rowed
And stumbled over brush and sands
Side by side yet far apart
To join the race much soon to start.

At darkness fall we thronged the fields
And keenly heeded calls of birds
Whose cheering songs had urged us on
With little more than distant hope
That races ran without some light
Would prizes yield though in the dark
And fortunes gained but for a while
Before the fruitage of the trees
And the grain of all seasons' end
Would the cold sweat of all reward
When races ran without some light
Would in delight soon come to end.

I on my part took to my heels
And scrambled on to distant hills
In dauntless strength and gallant strides
Unknowing what awaits afar;
The distance way beyond the view
That stars in darkness could not peer
To marshal contenders of this day
Through doom and gloom of bigotry
That tears the feet off men of fame
Off the pathways of our own race
In total darkness and disgrace
And in the blindness of your eye.

Before I Go Away

When I am grown
Past years of teens and tens of time,
I will in princely rule arise
Erecting towers on mountaintops
From which my septer and my rod
Will crush the helpless and the meek
For I in kingly power and fame
With none shall I stand to compare.

When I am grown in bounteous wealth
With hills of silver and of gold
Without concern for lowly folk,
Those poor my realms will never tread
On toes that peep through broken shoes
Without a sole to shield their foot
From thorns and thistles in their fields
On which my stock have long been grazed
To serve my guests in royal feasts
As subjects sing and dance for me.

When hungry crowds bow for my bread
My eyes shut not their lids in shame;
When I in kingly rule have grown
Beyond such loathsome poverty
Whose playmate I will never be
As long as my kingship holds sway
Before the sands of my own time
In trickling counts of years gone by
Draping my life in vanity,
The very day I fade away,
My fame on books shall find no page
For I have long lived but in vain.

Counting Time

Counting, and counting still I am,
The clouds that have since taken flight
In stormy times of ticking clocks
Whose call to rise awakened you
To cherish love that you and I
Had shared without a muted sigh
For all I had to you I gave
And traded love for your disdain.

Counting, and Counting will not cease,
The myriads of seasons gone by,
The sunsets that had come with rain
To wash away my tears in fear
That you would never look my way
Despite my yearning for the day
When you and I in one refrain
Would leap in joy in all our days
Before two flower wreaths they lay
On tombs on which good lovers lay.

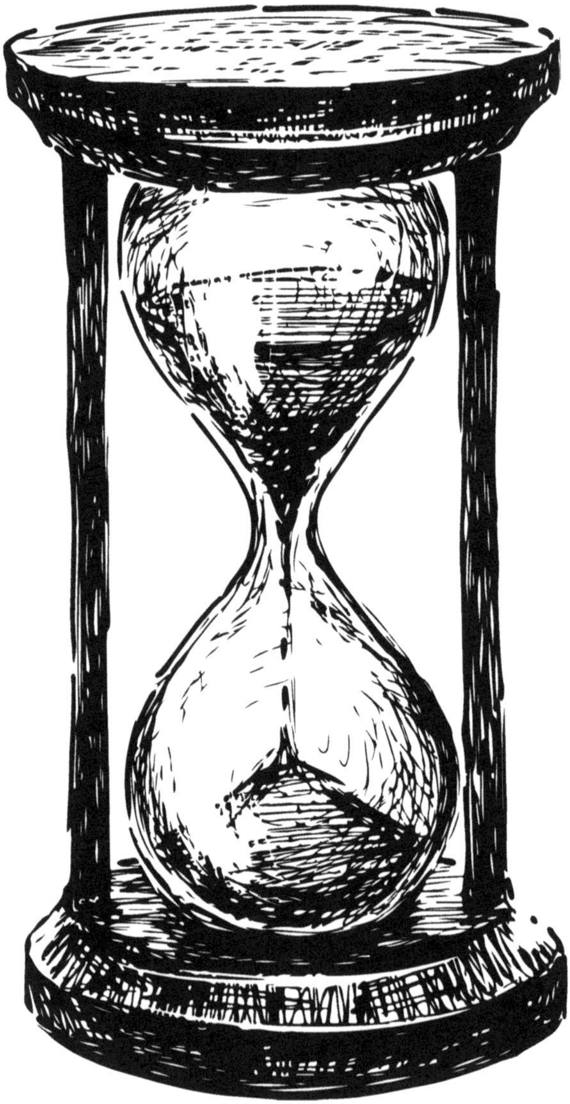

Dancing in the Rain

When rains came down in toddling pace,
We locked our arms in elbowed grips
And leaped in dance to rolls of drums
Whose beats lit flames in youthful eyes
As visions blurred by bounteousness
Would see no more than light of day
Beyond which no much future lay
For these our lands were most embraced
In spiritistic vulgaries
Without a care for nights and days.

When winds of heavens brought us rain
To nurture sprouts of healthy grain
And feed our rivers to their fill,
We raised our arms in thankfulness
To worthless gods we did not know,
Indulging in idolatry,
In spiritistic vulgaries
Without a care for nights and days.

But now that all the rain is gone
We turn to God and supplicate
For favours we do not deserve
As we, for countless nights and days,
Had wandered as we went astray
In pursuit of world's worthless gains
Before the dawn of truth's would light
Our roadway to hope in new day
When those that fell would rise again
To celebrate eternity.

Daring to Dream

I have had dreams time and again
Of trees with yields at season's end,
Rekindling hope in darkened nights
When neither mournful lonesome owl
Nor leaping flees in summertime
Would stir the storms in troubled souls
With whom I clang to yesterday
When roaring seas and tides of time
Washed all ashore on baren lands
Where broken dreams were laid to rest
And sowed as seed for future time
When all dared dreams would sprout and bloom
And give way to some new bright day
While all earth's woes would drift away.

Demons at Play

What sport for love demons contrive
With words designed to formulate
The rules to which they yield at play
With words of charm and lust as one
As though the heavens and the earth
Were urged to yield to their mischief
When spirits bound for hades bonds
Took choice brides from earth's moons and stars.

What sport these demons of today
Have for their bows and arrows aimed
As cupids in their tales and myths
Inflict deep wounds in lovers' dreams
To quench the thirst of devil's tongues
That lick their brides with firy flames
Before retreat to impotence
Reposed in tears of broken hearts?

Do maidens that you bear with pride
In all their awesome beauty laid
Take cautious strides on earth's pathways
That lustful demons of today

Their open arms they do not lay
And lure your youths to pasturage
With naked wolves and boisterous tongues
Embraced in latent treachery?

Do Let Me Be

Do let me be, pray let me be;
To be what storm is without rain,
What glaring sun is without light
Or yellow moon without a smile
On hidden faces of my days
As they peer down in muffled gaze
Amused by rodents in their race
To win the hearts of predators
To whose tunes they have danced in vain
To celebrate humanity.

Let me be, pray just let me be
The lonesome eyes that cannot see
Beyond the thought that we are one
While man and beast have taken stands
On platforms curved on treachery
As sky and earth where they are poised
Keep quaking, hungering for more
Than earth can give to feed its own
Whose leaders have long ran amock
Devouring what stands in their way

Despite promises that they made
To stop the tears of lowly beasts
That masquerade in their parade
To give them votes to reign all day.

Eye of the Storm

Is it the rage of angels' breath
With which you blew a fiery kiss
That stirred the flames that burn to-date
With grips of torment on my heart?
Is it you that I now behold
Or angels robed in nothingness
To stir the waters in my groin
That I with sons and daughters too
May populate the village folk
To raise a race of fallen souls?

What magic words had supple lips
That stand to guard a tongue so sweet
With which you had cruel love proclaimed
Oblivious of my feeble frame
That would not stand so passionate
As one to whom love was unknown
In strides of lonesome nights and days
With which I tread this dark terrain?

Do let me in eyes of more storms
Be borne to heights I hadn't known
Before you snatched my solitude
And robbed me of death, yes so close,
As I by tombs was gently drawn
To celebrate eternity
In blissful form of vanity
By which I'd be with clamps embraced
In arms of angels of your land
On which I tread in majesty.

Faces of Development

We see less faces on bright days,
Than in dark nights when peering eyes
Whose wounding gaze like question marks
Cast doubt on our own dignity
And camouflage the veils of shame
By which they drape our poverty
While skinny soldiers of our kings
March past on squares where we parade
As others leap in song and dance
To celebrate modernity.

These hands in toil and servitude
Have laid each brick upon a brick
Despite their hunger and their thirst
With which their numbers must contend
While building walls that barricade
The pathways to prosperity
As merchants with their tools of trade
Build bridges to their cloudless skies
By which our visions and our dreams
Are dwarfed and firmly held at bay.

Flowers that Wouldn't Bloom

Is it not true that love is mute,
With sunken eyes that do not see
The blobs of tears that drop and roll
Behind the mask of falling rain
To turn away the muffled dreams
Of lovers lost in vanity
Searching for flowers that wouldn't bloom
And watching trees that wouldn't grow
On banks of streams that wouldn't flow
To feed the seas that wouldn't roar
With tumbling tides that wouldn't rise
Despite their print on sands of time?

Is it not true that love's own bed
With prickly thorns and thistle spread
Would sting the sides of lovers ends
On which they droop or pick to brood
When there is nothing left to do,
When hopes and dreams have taken flight
To heights where kites and eagles dare,
To perch and nest from night to day,
And stir the sunrise with a smile
Which wakes the flowers that wouldn't bloom?

Is love the embers and the coals
That thaw the chills of rampant woes
When friends in hatred crawl away
To nurse their limping hopes and dreams
And build low castles on their way
To lands where trees would never grow
On banks where waters never flow
To fill the oceans with no hope
As time and tides of love's new day
Wash home more flowers that wouldn't bloom.

Forgotten Dreams

Those nights and days have gone away
When raindrops danced on window panes
To celebrate matrimony
Of two in wedlock bound in vain
As passions by the wind were blown
To take him to lands far away
Where maidens' beauty unrestrained
Bore him to heights without restraint
To rob him of the love he gained
Though she in waiting had remained.

He sails to islands without names
And pitches camp through night and day
To celebrate debauchery
In arms of strangers who in haste
Rob him of silver and of gold
And passions that he tucked away
In selfish ventures of his day
Before they drew back in disdain
When they had nothing more to gain
Though she in waiting had remained.

The price of those forgotten dreams
Of young arms locked in tight embrace
Is more than lovers wish to trade
When hope and trust cannot be gained
By one who has been long enstranged
By souls in flight without some nest
For they would not come home again
To bury their forgotten dreams.

Give Me Time

Give me some time, a bit of time,
But keep eternity concealed
That I, in wisdom or in none,
May wallow in idolatry,
Bowed to riches laid at my feet,
Indulging in vain sanity
In a world known for lunacy
And fleeting spells of hopes and dreams.

Give me more time, a little time,
That like a piece of good fortune
I might trade life for vanity
With demons of my heart's desire
For wealth in gold, unbounded fame,
Besieged by greed and draped in shame
Despite the truth that sits in wait,
Untold in tales of muted tongues.

Give me no time, not one more time,
That death for life I might not trade
Except for love of youthful brides

When truth stripped off its cloak of time
Reveals the ills of humankind
Whose race is drunk with wealth and fame
Without a vision or a thought
Of days to come at break of dawn.

Here Comes Democracy

Man has for seasons without end
Fought battles with their kings and counts
For freedom and for liberties
From reason and prosperity
And draw blood from their princely seed
To quench the thirst of ghostly greed
In rituals lined up in parade
To celebrate democracy.

Here comes your yearned democracy
Decked in colours of your bride
Who rides on chariots that you draw
As whips on your back rise and fall
For horses have no strength to rise
Or withstand the weight of their reins
With which you are drawn to your fate
By champions of democracy.

Will you in some good sense remain
In shackles and chains of their whims,
In poverty and in disease,
In prayers that will never be heard

To grant your wishes made in vain
While your trodden nations remain
Barren, lifeless without a grain
As you hail your democracy?

Now here comes your democracy
Decimating both friend and foe
In her hunger and in his thirst
While in fake glory and in praise
You dance to horns and rolling drums
In your lost battles and in strife
For the elusive bread and wine
As you hail your democracy.

If Only

If only you would sing some more
With magic words that mountains move
To blaze trails on which I would race
As I to you would come in haste
With seeds of life that I would bear
To light your roadways in the night
And shelter you from stormy winds
That have for eons in turbulence
Blown off the candles you had lit
To give life to your hopes and dreams.

If only drums would roll in song
Of lyrics known to lovers' hearts
That I might hear and touch and feel
The warmth that only words embrace
As tales of love or lust are told
To baren hearts that bear no fruit
Despite the seasons' sweet refrain
In praise of lovers of our day.

If Only I Could Have My Way

If I were poised in awe and might,
Would I view mankind in delight
Despite their twisted thoughts and deeds
Or would I like a gast of wind
Wipe out their fondest memories
Of paradise long lost in time
And plague them with woes, faithless foes
For whom there can be no restraint?

If I were waves that rove the seas,
Would I all their vessels upturn
And toss their wrecks on crags at shore
Whose jagged teeth have yawned for more
Of man consumed in decadence
Without a tear shed in regret
As light and darkness bear witness
To wickedness beyond compare?

If only I were blazing coals,
Their hearts and mind I would consume
And scorch to ashes life and limb
With which they scheme debauchery

On alters that they had once laid
To sacrifice to formless gods
Of wood and silver and of gold
To which they prostrate but in vain.

If I were enthroned as their king,
What mercy would I ever show
To faithless humans and their chiefs
With whom they have always communed
To perpetrate gross sacrilege
In festivals at harvest time
When full moons light their lush courtyards
On which their virgins danced to songs
Sang through the beaks of wicked owls
And tongues of demons while in flight?

If Only It Would Rain

See how much this my hair is grayed,
As feet without a sandal treads
An earth most robbed of fruit and grain
Long known to birds and man and beast
Before the baren sands of time
Lay down sad history at our feet
To watch us live from hand to mouth
While kings and princes of our day
Robbed orphans of their rationed bread
And feasted every night and day.

We toil in gold mines all our days,
Unstopping oil fields on the drill
For precious waters in its flow
To foreign lands without a sigh
Though wealth of these lands have been drained
To build those castles that you see
On those green hills we cannot scale
To dine with princes of our day
Whose guards have laid a walled blockade
On this our village five decades
Through which we've lived bereft of rain.

Toss just one grain our way we pray
That we might have a seed to sow
And do let dark clouds give us rain
That we may live to see the day
When gnawing hunger and disease
To which the sovereign in parade
Has stopped his ears and closed his eyes
Despite our wailing as we pray
For seasons when there would come rain
To bring back life to us again
And cleanse this land of maladies
From which the sovereign never ails.

In Angel's Arms

I couldn't help but shield the moon
With leads of gold as was her eyes
That matched the beauty I behold
As tender arms of feathered touch
Bathed me from woes of yesterday
Before the dewdrops of this day
Refreshed my thirsting sullen heart,
Igniting hope in our rebirth.

The dark-skinned angel of my day
Has two pearls fashioned for her eyes
With embers fit to light my way
With beams of love that never fade
Despite the signs of season's end
When coals of lovers would grow cold
As they prospect for gold to hold
In place of angels of their day.

The feathered touch of Angel's arms
That locked us in scented embrace
To heal heart's turmoil of the day

Was soft as songs of rested wind
Whose whispers urged us to repose,
Take refuge in our hopes and dreams,
Despite the clawing whirling winds
From which I'm shielded in her arms
Day after day, night after night,
Till all our dreams have come to roost.

In Awe of Gods They Do Not Know

When morning comes again tonight,
Its naked eye in poise to pry
Into this world that has no face,
That knows no shame or tempered pride,
By whom would daring voice be raised
Or laughter peel through restless clouds
On which your princes as their realm
Erect more castles in the air?

When morning comes to cleanse the sky
Of the foul breath of angered owls
Do they not see their day as done
And take to flight before the rage
Of multitudes whose voices raised
Consumes the heirs to lofty thrones
On which their kings have long held sway
Before their tumbling mountains grey?

When wheels of change are turned about
Their sons and daughters in their pride
Point fingers to the cloudless sky

And curse the gaping mouth of hades
For whom they blame their tragedies
As acts of gods they do not know
Or see in visions prophesied
In awe of gods they do not know.

In Memoriam

They laid our love in comely rest
From vexing beams of zealous stars
And teasing smiles of curious moons
Below which she walked in her days,
Night after night till break of day
When coloured life, like mist in flight,
Appeared just for a bunch of days
But disappeared in youthful haste
For what we are is quick to fade
While others quake in fear, in tears.

She has not died, not for one day,
Though gloom of realm in which she lies
Stands in the way of one bright day
When those reposed in memories
Will shed off sands and drops of dew,
Aroused from sleep by sovereign calls,
To wipe the tears we shed in vain
While mourning those that never die
Except in fogs of sunset days
When demons call on us to play.

But He will call and she will rise
And He will mold with His own hand
The priceless vessels of new day
When He will roar and we must quake
To cast off death for ever more
And pick new lives in paradise
That we might live at His command
As precious molds of His bare hands.

In Praise of Angels of My Day

In praise of angels of my day,
With pride I pause to recollect
The decades through which she has grown
From childish touch to kiss my nose
To rainbow colours of her youth
Whose sapling grown in majesty
Is sang in Baba's prideful song
In praise of one that I behold
Without a murmur or a sigh
For she, in strides as long as mine,
Has walked the world in width and breadth
In search of wisdom she has gained.

Though Baba's thoughts have often strayed
In leaps and bounds, in memories
Of days when we would congregate
To dine and wine in humble ways
When Nina in her childish play
Would beck and call all to some dance
To glorify our maker's name
For benedictions in my days
With lustrous angels to embrace.

Let your abode so far away
Across calm seas I cannot sail
Repose in peace in my mind's eye,
In musings I always embrace,
Of love for Nina and for you
As dawns and nightfalls come and go
To usher you in patronage
To Baba's arms just one more time
That all our dreams in one accord
May come to fruit in merriment
When I would dine and wine again
With lustrous angels in parade.

In Solitude

This game of life that few have played
For gains with silver cannot trade
When self with peace preoccupies
With racing thoughts and myriad dreams
At which those lone, in solitude,
Gaze at more chests of precious gems
By which our years are best festooned,
Removed from world's society
In song and dance, in vibrancy,
By which our souls are least concerned
For joy and peace we do not find
In crowded streets or liquor dens
In which small talk is bought and sold,
Exchanged for priceless solitude
In which my verses are composed
On golden boards of solitaire.

In the Eye of the Storm

I bear quick storms, most turbulent,
And sought for shelter in your arms
But you, so cowed, you took to flight
While I embraced in thunderbolts
Dance to the lyrics in their roars;
Blinded by beauty in their Strikes
As wondrous music in the air
Was all there was for my embrace.

Yet you my soul and poetry,
My spiced and flavored cocktail drink
By which my thirst were often quenched
To stirr me off much solitude;
When like the moon that waves embrace
You pulled me close like your own breath
In song and dance on sandy shores
On which my feet had their hold found
In watch as ripples kiss the shore
As the day breaks with muffled dreams.

Beyond reach you have not remained
While I with mastless boats I sail
On stormy seas and starry nights
Despite my dream that all my days
You would restore my light in days
When twilight comes in majesty,
In song and dance bathed in new moons
To celebrate our love some more
As all your wishes and your dreams
I always will make them come true.

In the Name of Democracy

Behind downcast face of these crowds,
Beneath shadows of virgin woods,
Gallant angels with doom descend
And glower upon their brazened heads
Like demons clad in whirling winds
Well cast to stage Armageddon
Raring to swoop over their prey
And deal the nations tragic blows
For the sins of democracy,
The price that subjects have to pay.

When mournful tears like fountainheads
Besides the whimpers and the sobs
And sullen stares from mountaintops
Leave little to be said or done
As trumping feet of their own youth
Give way to murmurs in defeat
When votes are counted one by one

In sounds of real democracy,
It is then that sharp arrowheads
And flaming swords of mighty men
Commune with hateful multitudes
To vanquish foes of faithless kings
With whom in temples and courtyards
They bowed to gods and sacrificed
Their sons and virgins in their youth
In names of lame democracy.

In the Name of Love

Of love, they say,
Was priceless in the days gone by
Until the tradesmen of this day
Came bearing gems in open arms
Whose hold in matchless warm embrace
Sent lovers scrumbling for firm hold
On gold and silver in return
For plastic love on stock exchange.

Of ancient lovers, they would say,
Would court and cuddle not in haste
In patience that their years had known
When dewdrops waited for the sun to rise
Without a murmur in complaint
Though smouldered in the heat of day
When young and old alike would trade
Their love for maidens of their day
In cultured ways with dignity
Unknown to tradesmen of this day.

Of gold and silver they would say,
Give us and we will in return
Surrender all that we are worth
To harvest riches at the stock exchange
For love then known in days gone by
Finds warm embrace in fairy tales
Told to those schooled in their own ways
Who real love cannot celebrate
Because with theirs they would always trade
With those robed in hypocrisy.

In War and Peace

In times of peace man like a beast
His breed would feed with soaring greed
For lustrous silver and for gold
With which his cities and roadways
Are laid and robed in majesty
To match the beauty of these lands
On which the fruitage of his works
Give life to hatchlings and the sprouts
By which their youth is signified
Before consumption by the sword.

In times of war, as tales have told,
The sons and daughters of their land,
Were famed for what they did not know
And sang in lyrics of their youth
In praise of princes of their day
While sun and stars had closed their eye,
Embracing earth in doom and gloom,
As ripples of life bowed in death.

In days when standards had been raised
And war cries rang in battlefields
To consummate man's lunacy,
Your voices rose to supplicate
For rain that only peace begets
As though his lands by demons reigned
Had turned its wrath on human race
With plagues of war and pestilence
Dealt with ill fingers of his kind
Before the tides of peace are born.

Let There Be Light

Do light a candle on my face
And peel off sun rays that I see
The glow that lights up your dark eyes
Whose grip on my own blinded eyes
Like molten clamp on finger tips
Hold as though you can't let go
The arms from which our dreams had strode
In pilgrimage unknown to rest
Until the nesting rock was known
To hearts locked tight in memories
Of days that we could not let go
Without the pain of losing you.

Bring sunrise to these old blind eyes
Whose curious questions posed in haste
Would shelter nothing unrevealed
Where love and hate in one embrace
With passionate kisses in reckless truth
That all is well though not quite so,
That you and I in love enslaved
Can bear lone fruits in barrenness

And give life to earth's new world
When springs of life burst forth once more
To sacrifice in multitude
Sons born of dawn and life's new day
When kingdom comes to reign the earth
And sanctify Jehovah's name.

Lost in Your World

The day you took me to your world
And placed my heart upon your stand
Where candle lights stood up to dance
In silent nights where winds don't blow
On baren fields where drums don't roll
And rivers stilled, never to flow,
Despite the storms of time gone by
Watched by wild birds and silent hills
Unmoved by trumpets friends had blown
To celebrate eternity
As maidens warmed by bread and wine
In walk so gay to imitate
The strides you took into my arms
To call to order hopes and dreams
That you would take me in such arms
As would have me lost in your world.

Love long Gained

The sound of chuckling crickets ring
In muted talk with little beasts
In whose communion we delight
As hand in hand we walk the way
While nighfall looms from hills on high
To welcome us and celebrate
The bond of love for which we die
And rise again when the day breaks.

Thus far we are still on our way
In search of shores and sandy bays
On which our anchors hold in wait
For love to stir our hearts again
And consummate rebirth of days
In search of which we sail in haste
To find these harbours not designed
To give us warmth in their embrace
Before we sailed to foreign lands
On which true love unknown remains.

I hear their laughters and their groan
As lovers come and go their way
Without a murmur in complaint
For life's vain leisure comes as host
By whom true love remains unknown
To beasts of sizes, shapes and heights
Whose measure I cannot attain
For love of mine I have long gained
And lowered sails on humbled plains
On which our love we consummate
To give new life to her domain.

Love's Hiding Place

You cannot hide your love from me
Or shield your heart from arrowheads
Of passion's valiant escapades
By which our love was decked and crowned
As though set for a pilgrimage
To barren lands beyond the seas
On which you like lone mastless boats
Were turned and tossed by stormy winds
As you attempt to hide your love
And tear to shreds your hopes and dreams.

I have this while in waiting been
For your return in modish haste
That you and I may reunite
Far from your love's dark hiding place
That we may like dawn waits for day
And morning dew awaits shy dawn
On the green side of childish grass
Before sun's rays draw good cheer
In which we set to celebrate
The love that you and I had known
Before concealment in lost dreams
In which my love was always laid.

But lo! What tidings are in hand,
Borne on wings of unspoken words
And beads of tears that you have drawn
While I in lonesomeness retreat
In hope that winds of some good day
Would whirl away the stinging thought
That you were gone far, far away,
Without a hope or wish or dream
That you and I would reunite
To share the love that lies entombed
For years concealed in barren dreams
In which my love was always laid.

My Turn at Play

We hid and sought in childish play
Before the sun withdrew its face
To give way to moon's charming looks
That summoned each to sheltered heaths
On which we scrambled for wild fruits
As Mama's pot simmered some more
While promising to fill our souls,
Rekindling hope for empty hands,
As stars in heaven closed their eyes
And opened doors to distant dreams
On which tomorrow like sowed seed
Would grow as tall as fantasies
On which our castles stood erect
Before the truth would dawn on us
That wealthy kings of nowadays
Would nothing share with destitute
Except the crumbs of molded grain
On which we gnawed in poverty,
While giving few another chance
To let them take their turn at play.

Prosperity

When one in grave want and in gloom
Picks a coin from one's yawning purse
And seeks protection by his kind,
The crowds in anger would give chase
And break his neck on cornerstones
Then wash their hands on reedy pools
Where thieves and witches were interned
To teach them lessons of the day.

But when the lordships of their day
Force open chests in treasury
And all their silver and their gold
Is wheeled to distant hills by day,
The crowds in envy and in awe
Sing praises to their lords and kings
And pray that crumbs would fall again
That they might share like sacrament
When royal tables are all laid
To celebrate prosperity.

Season's End

Night after day seasons parade
Paving roadways for life in vain
As seeds and fruit strive in their day
To give life to mankind and beast
In days of bounteous harvest time;
In years of want, of nakedness,
Despite man's zeal to supplicate
For tranquil times that would not cease.

But seasons too have their due say
To faithless mortals of our day
On whom gale winds in wrathful blows
Inflict on all due recompense
For sins of fathers and of sons
As though with billows of their breath
Would wish away their vise and shame
With which mankind has long been plagued.

Do tell me, oh! When winters' end
Would come to spring as summer times
Embrace this race in timelessness
That all may rise to life again
From seed to fruitage of new days
When all in choral voices ring
To celebrate these seasons' end.

Talking to Me

I talk to me through night and day
When I rise up, when I lie down,
To hear the wisdom of my mind
That taunts the folly of my age;
I hear voices of history
Casting doubt on mine own resolve
To pick up seeds of puzzled dreams
Whose visions have my hope embraced
As darkness falls to close the gates
To frames of time where I have laid.

I talk to me and hear the tones
Of words like flowing rivers deep
Where sunken heroes of my day
Washed off their courage and their pride
To land where masters and their slaves
Have suited garments just the same
Like beggars who their fortunes bear
Without a murmur or a cry
As mighty foes from distant lands
Rob all of treasures they had claimed.

I talk to me through sun and rain
To feel the stormy winds brush by
And lap to dry the tears I shed
When earth and sky had teamed as one
In bundles of conspiracy
To bring an end to piece of mind
And plague my visions and my dreams
With blinding shadows cast around
At times when voices from within
Would wail and scream like mine own foes.

Tell Me Tales

Tell me tales that are never told
In honest tongues well known to man
Or sang in songs of curse or praise;
Let me feel your naked breath
That bears your empty words of love
Cited in shreds of ancient books
That lie in archives of your filth
Awaiting moments when deceit
Embroidered in your scented speech
Find lodging in my wary ears
As in my heart they find no place
For love told of in fairy tales.

Talk to me without an embrace
Or plastic smiles upon your face
That I might see that curtained look
Bathed in cold tears amid my fear
That I, in naked honesty,
Have cast ashore your rampant dreams
To hold me captive in a wilderness
That knows no lure to love or hate

Despite the tales that you have told
In search of your soul's resting place
In temples that you desecrate
With decors of your schooled pretense.

Tell Them!

By Evelyne W. Kimani

Tell them I have been there and seen
The treacherous road that I have trod;
Tell tales of bumps from which I hurt
That they might know from where I come;
Race to the ends of this wide world,
To corners of this globe in all its craze,
That you might tell them so they hear
Of arduous journeys of my day.

Tell them I tried, maybe in vain,
Even though I had given all
With nothing left for fellowman
To ask of me in honesty;
Tell them I tried to remain strong,
Though weakness in its shameless might
Subdued me often and for whiles
Sprinkled with joy, tears, fears and dreams.

Tell of my greatness, of my might,
Of strength to bear myriads of woes,
But do recall my fears and tears,
The battles that I won and lost
Despite endurance through dark days
Of which my tales are to be told,
Of woman bearing spears and shields
To conquer self and history.

The Aftermath

The senseless wars that man has waged
And flames of those that once had lived
Have smouldered into vanity
To seek refuge in solitude,
Embraced in arms of lifelessness,
Without a whimper or a tear
For those who long had lived in pain
Much like waves born of raging seas
That disimate both friend and foe
In tidal motions of their day.

The aftermath of war and peace
Whose borders faded, undefined,
Elude the dreams of those in youth
Had visualised a paradise
In which without sweat born of toils
Would pluck the fruitage of their dreams
From trees on lands that none had tilled,
Soils sown with seeds of fantasy.

What sets apart man and the beast
Except vile spirit and the greed
With which he sets out to consume
His seed and grain, both fruit and tree,
In times of war and times of peace
Oblivious of tomorrow's needs
When grain and rain defy his pleas
To give life to his newly born
Whose fate has long been well defined
By aftermaths of war and greed –
As all their visions and their dreams
Lie entombed in dark history.

The Bitter Fruitage of Their Reign

Their sons were born in tides and turns
Before their world became of age
And left to fend in scanty rains
And make the best of sour fruitage
From which wild seeds have come to bloom
To give forth demons much enraged,
Whose lives in seasons of distress
Endure tempestuous circumstance
That shapes the form of wickedness
With which man dines to celebrate
The birth of sons of rotten fruit
By which the earth is bred and fed.

They whirl and wind in twists and turns
In violent gales across the sea
To procreate more wickedness
Espoused in nations where they reign
With iron fists and arrowheads
To signify sovereignity
Of kings and princes you behold
From sea to sea, from hills and dales,
Across the plains on which no grain
Has grown for decades of their reign.

But would they go because they pray
To lifeless gods of wood and stone
To whom they bow in blinded faith
And offer blighted sacrifice
Of lame lambs charred by thunderbolts
To blot out tides of decadence
With which their shores like tables laid,
As they revolt but all in vain,
In waste of silver and fine gold
Which they have in their altars laid.

The Cockroach Dance

These burial grounds on crevasses
Hold generations of our kind
From womb to tomb in swarms and throngs
That rise and fall to pesticides
When man sends beastly fumigants
To decimate the vermin race
Without a trace in history
But for the sounds of muted moans
Before our seed would sprout again
To populate our cockroach dance.

We took on life in faecal waste,
In drainage gutters of this day,
In hope that roaches of our day
Would colonise their large estates
And bring man down with pestilence
In place of massive weaponry
With which they seek their own demise
Without a fleeting thought or muse
While roaches pray for nights to come
When hips wriggle in cockroach dance.

The Cost of Love?

Do tell me what love you have known
And sing in lyrics you compose
If not sounds of mediocrity
Adorned with vile naked pretense
With which you stretch a thousand arms
To hold me shackled in embrace
In view of those at marketplace
With whom your love is for a trade.

Come, tell me what love you have gained
From merchants whom you once embraced
In return for their treasured gold
And chambers in which you were laid
To dine and wine to satiety
Before their noble entourage
Had left your cities at daybreak
To distant lands in fairy tales.

Oh! Come and let these mine own eyes
Behold the embers in your face
Before they smothered in the winds
While you in youth and in old age

Stood spent in dance to muted songs
To which you swayed in distant dreams
Of riches for which you had preyed
Unknown to lovers of my race.

The Day You Went Away

The day you rose and sailed away,
And wished our nights and days away,
Awash with tears, with much to say,
When all my hopes and dreams like hay
On broken altars they were laid
While you and I like childish rain
Had on cold grass our hazed heads laid
In wait for dawn from distant bays
From which the sunrays of good days
Would bear good tidings on this day,
I couldn't but much wished I'd pray
To mute the memories in bright caskets laid.

The Earth Will Sing

By Evelyne W. Kimani

One day, and soon, the Earth will sing;
It will break open into song
Of valiant youth and old alike,
Of mighty rich and trodden poor;
The earth will sing of endurance
In wars we fought and battles won,
A hymn in words of doom and gloom
That tell of tales of single moms,
The anguish of husbands abused,
The piercing cry of the unborn,
And young lives dashed in cruelty.

The earth when poised will tell it all
And break its silence in a song
To tell the sad tales of those aged
Yet tucked in lonesome lives to death,
To tell of homeless souls in need
Of food and shelter day by day,
Of the lone child with none to love
And mourn those that died with clean hands.

I sit and wonder if some day
The earth will pay for sinless blood
Shed on its face in tyranny
Day after day as she laments
The strife and pain of her own sons
Whose love for brother have long lost
As told in songs that this earth sings,
Of those whose footprints in their wake
Tell tales of hatred, of no hope,
As love of many has grown cold
To join the earth in sad refrain

The Lunacy of Love

Love like a kite that wouldn't soar
But loom like shadows in our trail
Would lurk behind the best of times
When high and low tides drift ashore
Bearing dreams sawn in tears of joy
In hearts ill fated most of times
As love's lunatic pleasantries
Plague lovers in their lunacy.

But what is love without the pain
Of facing bear realities
That transient feelings they call love
Like swirling winds and rising mist
Would drift away in dawn of time
When fools robed in bright fantacies
By which they are preoccupied
Would soon call off their pilgrimage
To realms where demons now hold sway
And rein unbridled beasts called love.

The Price of Peace

Not for your silver or your gold
Is world peace sold or is exchanged
In marketplaces of our day
That you may as a king hold sway
As your young seed is always slain
At the altars of selfish gain
While your own bellies unrestrained
Have consumed our bread and wine.

All your peoples in one refrain
Raise high their voices but in vain
For the prospects of your own gain
Will never yield to their campaign
To bring healing to their domain
Over which you have held sway
After more battles of their day
Gave way to your treacherous reign.

The Sunset of Our Day

The seasons through which we have strayed,
The dewdrops and the touch of rain
Whose waters in your thirst embraced
To soothe us wen the scorching sun,
Had robbed us of the youthful zest
With which we skipped and hopped and jumped
On fields on which we were at play
Before the sunset of our day
Had brought an end to childish play
As youth gave way to seasoned age.

Perhaps that is all we have lost;
The face of colours on parade,
The tales of warriors and their brides
Brought home with stocks from distant plains
With song and dance in praise of hills
On which we stood and live or died
So that green grass can grow again
On pasturage on which we grazed.

Then comes the wisdom we disdained
And tufts of hair that now has grayed
As seasons that gave us some rain
Give way to bare sands at our feet
On burial grounds on which our lads
Lie silenced by dark history
Of ravaged fields laid desolate
By chieftains enthroned in our day.

The Vanity of Love

What would I do when seasons bloom
To face a dream in times of gloom
With empty stares at nothingness
But lustrous eyes where beauty lay
Compounded in their tenderness
With which her vision was pronounced,
In glowing love without an end
Attuned to songs of broken hearts,
Engraved on memoirs not yet penned,
Except in tears that I had shed
When demons in their treachery
Lay sheltered in our shattered dreams.

What can one's soul in whirling winds
Hold on when wicked storms in rage
Tear off masks of our masquerades
And light our eyes in full display
Of love professed yet all in vain
In naked words of emptiness
That robs us of our precious gems
Which lie concealed in honesty
Before the rupture of some day
When love and hate are robed like priests.

The Vanity of Man

If I were star or sun or moon,
Would I shed light on poor man's brow
And light his paths to give him hope,
And if I did, to what avail
For this mankind in darkness looms
And gropes as though a spell long cast
Has brought his works to nothingness
As man's labors are all in vain.

If mine own form were of a bee,
Would I his pallet seek to please
With honeycombs of my own charms
And drawn from hives he cannot craft
Or hoist to rest on heightened realms
To ward off rodents that have gnawed
The waning hope and smoldered dreams
Of sons and daughters borne in vain?

If I were poised like thunderbolts,
Would I not strike with just one blow
To dash his kings to smithereens
And cleanse this land of shameful greed

With which they graze on hills and fields
Like monstrous beasts that have consumed
All grain from fields that have been tilled
By sons and daughters borne in vain.

If torrents were my chosen form,
Would I with care wash all those tears
Off faces shameless for their deeds,
Or flow in brooks to quench their thirst
While elders squart to defacate
On fountainheads from which their springs
Gave life to sons and cultured beasts
Born of their daughters, all in vain?

The Winds of Change

When seasons come and seasons go,
The chilling winds and trickling rains
Descend on fields where innocence
Embraced in youthful solitude
Bow down in prayer for happier days
When green fields in their spring and bloom
Tell tales of joyous festivals
When when those infirmed and sound of limb
Rose up to dance to humming drums
Whose beats in legions on parade
Rose moon and stars to celebrate
The yields of grain at harvest-time.

When winds of change on hills and plains
Sweep with a chilling ghasts in haste,
No hand of man or demons wave
Would turn the tide of rising seas
Whose waters lap and grace the shores
On which no children ever played
Since man and beast in one accord
Had plagued the land with pestilence
That comes with every princely reign

Of hungry kings robed in bright greed
For trappings of their sovereignty
By which our lands are baren laid.

The Wind Storm in Conspiracy

When gathering storms in one accord
Have urged to battle earth and wind
In all their pomp and majesty
As raindrops cheered and jeered all meak
While drumbeats rolled to celebrate
The breaking waves as sails on masts
Arising in their victory
Amid the scrambling crawling beasts
That fumbled for a hold in vain
When winds and storms in one accord
Had bind farewell to sands and dunes
On which we stood without a speech.

Yet you and I would in refrain
Without a whisper in complaint
Hoist sails in pomp to celebrate
The sailor's tales from distant lands
Where you and I had sought refuge
Before the windstorms and their sons
Had all our daughters' fruits partake
In brides and spoils of their own fate

While muffled mothers in dismay
Gave in all hope in despair
And let their voices congregate
To mourn the living and the dead.

What then is this our hope and fate
When windstorms of this night and day
Our hopes and dreams would wash away
Without a murmur in restraint
That we may on our part delight
In sons and daughters of our day
When suns and moons without bare grace
Would darken days to doom and gloom
Without a glimmer of sun's ray
That brings good tidings to our race
For which this decade and its day
Has striven for mean mastery
To salvage broken hopes and dreams
And bring new life to more dark days
Though hope is laid on broken dreams
Borne on bare hands of liberty.

So, what have you on sickle's end
Held sway on harvest season's end
To satisfy the hungered race
With ripened fruit or well fed grain,
Without a voice raised in complaint,
Because none his wise hoe had raised
To weed this land of pestilence
And heal our hills of wounded pride
With which we are preoccupied
Come sunrise and when sun goes down
Without a hint of days gone by
Or hail and praise of seasons end.

To Love and Hate

I have long loved and learned to hate
The bitter and the sweet as one,
The gusts of winds and calming breeze
With which our lives are bone ashore
From distant lands where we were born
Before young dawns and old sunsets
Gripped tight all time and ticked away
Like clocks by which our love stood timed
Before cold blizzards fed with hate
Blew you and I in turbulence
To distant seas where sobs of rain
Swamped all the feelings we espoused
In love and hate that you and I
Have known through time and timelessness
That marks the plight of human race
By whom our candles were long blown
To usher in the emptiness
Where love and hate as twins embrace.

To Those that You Shall Say Goodbye

Do not be wise in your own eyes
Like fallen angels in skyways
Of transient passions for a day
Before you turn to say goodbye
As mind and heart are led astray
To worthless shelters made of hay
And plastic smiles of treacherous maids
With whom the demons copulate
To herald kings that your lands reign
Before they turn to say goodbye.

Do not be poised or your voice raise
In royal courtyards of the wise
Whose ears and eyes through countless days
Have known all that you have to say,
So do not be wise In your eyes
Lest by serpents you be embraced,
But hold and keep your peace of mind
And then do turn and say goodbye.

Vessels of Broken Dreams

Do heed to winds that grown and blow
Across the plains on which you grazed
To bring you hope and light your dreams
In colours of lost paradise
And yet, in greed and faithlessness,
You stare and gaze in disbelief
That sons and daughters of this land
Can stir to life both friend and foe
By whom these mountains and those hills
Were poised in stature and in form
Of colours of lost paradise
Before the bowels of your land
Devoured the truth, the right and wrong,
And whirled you into decadence
With which your fruitage and your seed
Feed demons to whom you now bow
Oblivious of gross wickedness
With which this land is decked and draped
On burial grounds on which now lie
Dry vessels of your broken dreams.

Waiting for Grass to Grow

I sat to wait for grass to grow
As mournful streams of trickling brooks
Recounted time when man and beast
Had by the waters of their springs,
For nothing paid in gratitude
Or in return for life so gained,
Were quenched when withered limbs were raised
To supplicate in savagery
As stars and moon in majesty
Had watched their worthless history
Go down their books of life and death
Scripted in mucky sands of time;
But nothing stirred on baren ground
On which lay buried hopes and dreams
Of plains once moist with morning dew
In which the serpent and the bee
Had bathes their youth to adulthood
Before the demons of our age
Had all life's foliage pruned and scorched
To recreate more misery.

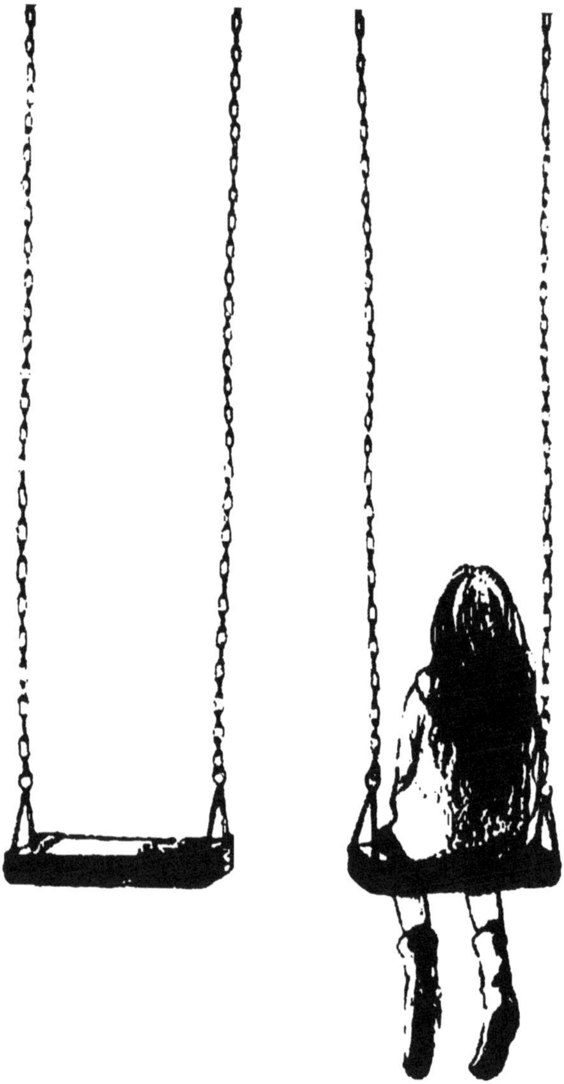

Waiting For You

I tell the tales of pillow's day
While on your bed I lifeless lie
In wait for knobs of doors to turn
And welcome faces I have seen
At times in pensive looks and fear
That reigns supreme in all your days
When faces drooping lost in thought
Took stock of moments we have shared
When in my arms you placed your head
And lay your fleeting dreams to rest.

Would you today like many days
Give way to tears encased in fear
Like racing wolves out in the wild
Before daybreak grinds them to halt;
Will you this night as those gone by
Cling to your memoirs while I gaze
With helpless looks on this my face
On which your teardrops must remain
In warm embrace and solitude
That only pillows can supply
When muted nights and lonesomeness
Hold you in mean captivity?

If life as human were my fate
I wouldn't trade my thread for it
Or raise my fist in victory
To celebrate humanity
Whose woes and foes I have well known
From writings penned in history
Through which I bore the weight of thoughts
And licked the sweat of your worn brow
Before your daybreak, I would hope,
Would bring you solace as I wait.

But I, a pillow, I remain
Embroidered in extravagance,
Stuffed in feathers of great lakes
Whose waters cannot bathe your pain
Or quench the thirst of your own greed
While I would nothing ask of you
Except that you at dusk return
That I may soothe your broken hearts
And give you comfort in the nights
Before your daydreams would come true
As I await your quiet return
Into my yawning lifeless arms.

Wars Without End

For days on end, wars without end,
Mankind in strife to decimate
Would rise in vain and fall in pain
When none would brother's wounds do bind
Or broken soul with potions cure
As nations bleed and none would heed
The clarion calls to bond in peace
When gold and treasures of their day
Are squandered much in weaponry
To wage more wars without entail.

We waged our wars but none had won
For decades come and decades go
To decimate our brotherhood
So we might reign on burial grounds
Where fallen heroes have been laid
With none to stand and sing their praise
For all our sons have long been slain
By wicked angels that hold sway
With subjects that would in parade
Join hands with demons of their day.

We have endured to see this day
When darkness looms in statelessness
As man like beasts has gone astray
And brandished swords in rage to slay
Without a moment of restraint
Despite their wailing and their cries
That he might reign on burial grounds
Where fallen warriors have been laid
Without a headstone or a tomb
On plains beset with wickedness.

Wartime Dreams

I have had dreams, my wartime dreams,
That gnawed me to the very bone,
The last of gifts in casket draped
For mothers who had known good days
When we on their frocks tugged and played
Before these wars broke out again
For reasons that I do not know
Why man his fellow man would slay.

I have had dreams these last few days
As those in battlefields would gaze
Without a vision or an eye
To see the evil in our eyes
As all our sons and daughters urge
To charge and decimate their young and old
All in the name of liberties
Encased in minds of wickedness

I had more dreams these last few days
Embraced in nightmares of our day
When nobles took hold of our reins
And herded us to destiny

In which we in our tombs have laid
Without a whisper as we turn
To look our history in the face
Dumbfounded as we take to flight.

Watching the World

I peer and see a naked world
In shades of days and gloomy nights
Of fame and shame and broken dreams;
Of barren fields where trees had grown
As reedy pools and boisterous brooks
In joyous trickles at their feet
Had quenched the thirst of rooted life
That quickened this society.

I see on mirrors of my eye
Angels that nurse the newly borne
And demons cuddling crowds in death
In burial grounds where grain had grown
Before proclaiming battlefields
To wage wars on the human race
And populate the decadence
With which this land has long been plagued.

I view more valleys and low hills
Robed and enriched with poverty
Despite the treasures long concealed
In chests of warriors and chieftains

Who roam the land in mighty strides
IN conquest over fellow man
Cheered on by throngs of hungry crowds
Consumed in gross idolatry.

What Would I See

If those with eyes still cannot see
The hidden mystery of mankind
Whose heart in hateful Masquerade
Have fane love for fellowman,
What then in your eyes would I see
But gathering clouds in cold pretense
And smiles in plastic formulae
In courteous haste for a goodbye?

In the perceptions of one eye
There stands a race in all its pride;
In the perception of both eyes
There lies the rot of humankind;
As man and beast enthroned as kings
Have stirred their seed in civil strife
Decked by dark shades of decadence
That quakes foundations of the earth
That will for sure descend to hades
As angels watch though least dismayed.

If I had eyes, what would I see
When kingdom comes as prophesied
To bring an end to wickedness
And sow new seeds of righteousness
From which will burst forth paradise
In coloured blossoms of new day
When you and I will live to see
A race of lovers in delight
As tears and pain have gone away
While we embrace eternity.

When I Am Gone

When I have gone away
Do not you be in haste to praise
Or judge me for my treachery
In which my wisdom lay concealed
So richly groomed in words and deeds
For where I go none can embrace
Or love one's own in good return
As I, postrate upon the earth,
Without a tear, without a smile,
Yet you, in your façade and veiled pretense,
Proclaim false love yet to be known
By one whose paths have led astray
To sandy shores where sun and moon
Have held at bay their countenance
Without a tear, without a smile,
To light the roadways for my foes.

When I grow Old

When sunset heralds end of time,
I will remember;
I will recall in one refrain
The drums that rolled at break of day
To stir up life and rouse from sleep
Quick springs of waters at our feet
To give life to our browning fields
And bring forth grain for man and beast.

When He in his millennial reign
Restores the earth to paradise,
I will remember;
I will recall the witnessing
And proclamations of good news
When all the woes and maladies,
As would wild ravens in one flight,
Would this our realm no longer plague.

When thunder lights my darkened eyes,
I would remember;
I would recall the songs we sang

As children dancing in the rain
From fertile clouds in bounteous yields,
Yet God's own children would not soak
In teardrops we could not withhold
In prayer that we would live again.

When Life Began

With healthful limbs I once had strolled
Along paths with their twists and turns,
Up hills and valleys I traversed,
Across life's bridges to my dream
In which one flower in its youth
Of dazzling colours of my day
Called forth the mighty sun to rise
And give life to my own delight.

Though curled up and cold on dark days
Our warm embrace would light our day
And brighten up her teary eyes
From which mine own would not depart
For fear that I would lose my hold
On beauty curved with elegance
Beyond the form of earthly brides
Untold in tales I had been told
In all the years that I had grown
For years before my life began.

Then came a lad and then a lass
To populate our family tree
Whose fruitage bounteous as could be
Have filled our hearts with gratitude
In times of plenty and of want,
For days and nights before the day
When Nina's birth would, one more time,
Breath life in Babu's new bright day.

When Mama Starts to Pray

We weathered raging storms and winds
To scale the heights on which we nest
While daring foes on land, at sea,
To raise their swords and deal more blows
Despite our mama's prayer for peace
To heal our fields so desolate
Without a blade of grass or grain
But thirsting yet for much more rain
When mama's prayers are heard this once
As daybreak's gaze in shyness draped
To hide her face from decadence
And wickedness of modern days
When Mama's prayers are never said.

When mama prays this one more time,
The birds that sang at dawn will mute
While pecking on the early worms
As ravens in communion leap
To bear good tidings far and wide
As green grass stirs beneath our feet
Without a care as drumbeats ring

While songs and dance unite as one
To celebrate season's rebirth
And the coming of a new day
When mama's prayers like frankincense
Would drape the air with matchless awe.

When mama prays for us again
And barking dogs their snarls restrain,
Let the communion of our voice
Ring like brave soldiers that lay siege
Around the scheming masquarades
By whom our youth lie low still slain
To lay a claim on victory
As rich rewards and wickedness
Bedeck their mansions and abodes
In festive days and boisterous nights
When mama's prayers were never said.

When Papa Cries

We never saw our Papa cry
Except in shadows of bare shrines
Where Mama's prayers were never heard
Despite her wails on barren lands
On which we played come summer time
When bounteous harvests of poor grain
Would fill storehouses in our dreams
Before she prays for rain again.

But Papa would not always cry
For fear that we would in refrain
Call on clouds that would bring no rain
As mists in their realms would hold sway
And deal more blows to thirsting plains
On which we grazed thin yawning beasts
In hope that land would yield fruitage
The day our Papa's tears bring rain.

These hands you see have tilled this earth
And stones we turned now lie prostrate
While farmished worms bereft of zest

Wriggle on clods of earth and sands
On which dewdrops would never perch
Despite our Mama's fervent pleas
And tears that stream down Papa's face
With eyes transfixed on distant dreams.

When the Rain is Gone

When stormy winds had picked their pace
And raindrop laden clouds in flight
Had on her face their burdens laid,
She had no care for fears or tears
For they would merely drift away
As fleeting thoughts of days gone by
Becloud dark nights with foggy dreams
That he and she had for long shared
Before the rains had gone away
To cleanse their heart's fond memories.

Before the rains had gone away,
They plowed and sowed on rich terrain
On which the blossoms of their souls
Had given life to happiness
Whose fruitage, much like history,
Had found no lasting resting place
In treacherous wombs of transient love
Traded by merchants of their day.

After the rains had gone away
And tools of love had long been laid,
They sang sad songs without refrain
Like lullabies to memories
That they as others laid to rest
In hope that rains would fall again
To quench the furious naked flames
That fuels cruel pains of lonesomeness.

When Will Day Break

No sun or moon will ever rise
In days or nights of continents
For sons and daughters have been slain
And sacrificed to worthless gods
Of wood and stone engraved with tools
Of treachery, yes, bigotry,
That in ferocious need and greed
We stand and fall like newly weds
Who overwhelmed by distant dreams
Have lived their lives in fairy tales.

No sun or moon will open eyes
To peer into this space and void
In which we lie in hopelessness,
In drunken slumbers of our days
That even history can't erase
Or cleanse our bloodstained hands again
As justice on the judgment day
Spells doom to this our land again
While we without hope rise and gaze
At leaders who have had their say
While lifeless masses of their day
Lie trodden and restrained at bay.

When will the sons and daughters rise
To harvest suns and moons again
That we at daybreak and at dawn
We would more sunsets hope to see
While grass on graveyards stir again
And flowers blossom in the rain
To yield sweet fruitage and good grain
That man and beast may comfort see
As suns and moons with stars in gaze
Would bring back life to us again?

Where is Love Laid?

No thousand drums or songs of praise
Can summon love from where it lay
Whether in dreams or heart's own bays
Whose waters storm our thoughts in vain
As love's legions of fantasie
Plot schemes just to intoxicate
Those gullible in life's domain
In which we meander and then stray
In search of love but all in vain.

Do tell me where your love is laid
Or merchants with whom I could trade
That I may find where mine while dazed
Had lost its way that I might pay
The price of loving unrestrained
Though all I had I gave away
In search of true love without pain
Yet without clues where my love lay
Whether entombed or in distress
Waiting for me to live again
And search for true love without gain,
Yet without docking on love's bay.

Where is the Fire?

Where is the RAGING LOVE LIKE flames
That charred our hearts in TURBULENCE
And licked our tears with fiery tongues,
The elusive warmth of waning smiles
When I knew you to be afraid
Of love from which we must refrain?

Where are the fragile pented words
That whispered music of our hearts
And stirred our souls to life again
In market places of this day
That dawns on silent listeners
By whom our songs were never heard?

Where are the youthful arms long gone
That clung to memories of each day
When moments as we said goodbye
Took you away in darkened nights
When I would die in need of you
Without a headstone for my tomb?

Where is my peace and resting place,
The baren womb of its embrace,
Where I must wait and refuge take
As you return in majesty
To bury this my lonesomeness?
Where is the fire, the words, the arms,
Where are our flames of love and hate
In which we always lay consumed?

Where Will We Go?

When we light bonfires on bare ground
On which we tread in confidence
Enchanted by their beck and call
While their own seed is tucked away
In castles built on foreign lands
Of which we hear in fairy tales
When merchants tug their wares in trade
For all the coins that we have gained
As wages paid to us each day,
Do we not turn back in dismay
In view of banquets that they lay
While we in strife and rampage rage?

Where will we go when storms of rage
Have washed ashore our broken dreams
As they in flight their refuge take
When all their battles that we fought
Leave this our land so desolate
With gaping fountains long gone dry
And bare grain stalks that without rain
Look up to mountains and dry springs
To give us hope that some new day
Will wastelands come to life again.

Where will your sons and daughters be
When princely kings in entourage
Parade their silver and their gold
On distant lands in majesty
While dogs and flies leap in delight
And lick your wounds on barren plains
On which your village was once poised
In silent watch for nights and days
As your own flames in pented rage
Devour your hopes and distant dreams;
To where will sons and daughters flee
In refuge from these yawning graves?

Whirling With the Wind

You can turn off the morning light
That flares for all to light their way
But would I not rekindle all
The embers that have closed their eyes
To shadows of their dark roadways
Trodden by most men in despair
For I have no share in their hopes
Nor in fortunes of broken dreams
Pursued by souls who nowhere go
For I must rise to live again.

If rains were to beat on my brow
And storms cast me far ashore,
Would I not pick my limbs and trail
The paths of wisdom and of truth
That man as I were born to live
And only die from time to time
To teach him how to live again
When seasons come for a rebirth
Of hopes and dreams that were espoused
In souls and spirits of the wise
Who have come to know who they are
Amid crowds whirling with the wind.

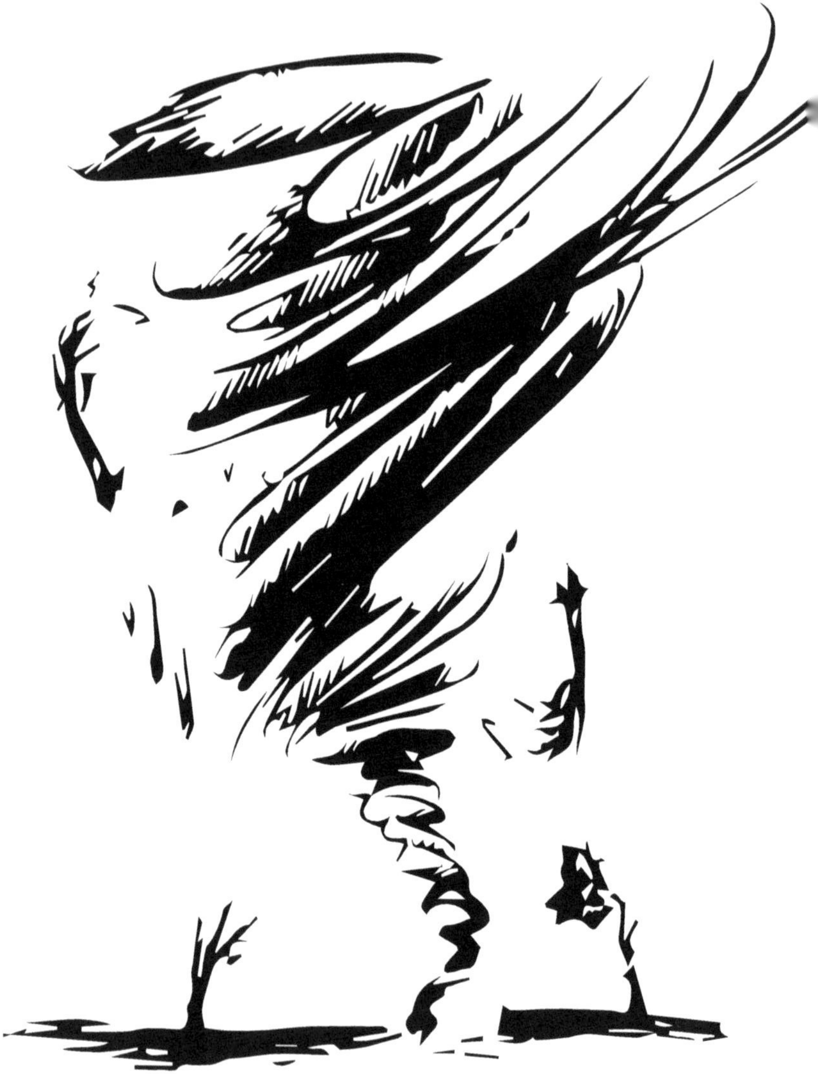

Who Am I?

Who am I in my vision laid
That I might in comfort repose
As I take count of good old times
And dark days at my feet have laid
For bridge upon which I must cross
To be what I have to become
When precious gems like earthenware
United by faint breaths of life
Are molded into what I am
Before being what a man must be?

Am I the wind on crested hills
That blows without one firm embrace
Or claim to own its lost pathways;
Am I the eyes that have beheld
Much beauty though without a hold
Or arms with which I could regain
Elusive pleasures of each day
Despite the charming smiles in gest
On lips that eyes without a tongue
Cannot moisten in gratitude
Or tell the tales of broken dreams
Before becoming man again.

Am I the storm that stirs from sleep
On baren fields where lovers lay
Before quiet whispers in refrain
Would quicken them to life again?
Is man the voice that speaks to me
From deep within a troubled soul
For which no cure have wise men found
Nor magic spells demons contrived
TO sow the seeds that peace of mind
Would nurture to maturity
To make a man from smithereens
And break the chains of solitude?

Who will You mourn?

Whom would you mourn of our lost race
Worth of one's song in praise or name
For good deeds towards those in need
In selfless love of brother's soul,
In times of ills of world's design,
When woes commune with friend and foe
In feasts laid on their burial grounds
To celebrate lives laid in vain
On yawning altars of this day
When those that live know they will die
And that their dreams are all in vain
Unless they rise to live again
And bear good fruit in paradise
When there would be none to be mourned,
And these old things have passed away,
To herald realms and sovereignty
When princely kings and queens that reign
Would bring to life those we had laid.

Who would you mourn among those laid;
The thief, the witch, the prideful priest,
Whose ways no demon would surpasse
To glorify dark cathedrals
Beset by plagues and decadence
As falsehoods held sway over truths
About the living and the dead
With whom they claim to have communed
Despite internment underfoot
Where worms and maggots grip their prey
Until those in memorial tombs
Would hear the call and rise again
To celebrate eternity
As pain and death wed history?

Would God Send Us Rain?

Would God in His benevolence
Send us more rain or pestilence
For the decadence of this race
Has taken root on fields like grain
And brought reproach to humankind
Who in one blow come to an end
And give way to its season's end
Before its seed would rise again
When God his mercies would apply
And give life to this race again?

See how those greedy filthy drains
Would for their own accumulate
Things worthless yet they drag in tow
And cling on in a warm embrace
The produce of insanity
In which mad men like beasts delight
Before maladies' mighty blows
Strike them down into lifelessness
And bring an end to their own race
To whom our God would still send rain.

But by whom would these beasts be mourned
If not by demons of their day
With whom they often congregate
To scheme in malice and in hate,
To quench a thirst that would not end,
With streams and rivers long gone dry
In fear of man's own wicked race.
Whose days long counted near their end
Before the Sovereign from his throne
Holds back the clouds that gave us rain.

What then for man so desolate;
What would become of serpentines
Whose seed his venom has consumed
And bedeviled this human race
Now destined to succumb to plagues
And woes more of their own design
Before the Sovereign from His throne
Determines to sow righteous seed
To raise a people for his name
And never fail to give us rain?

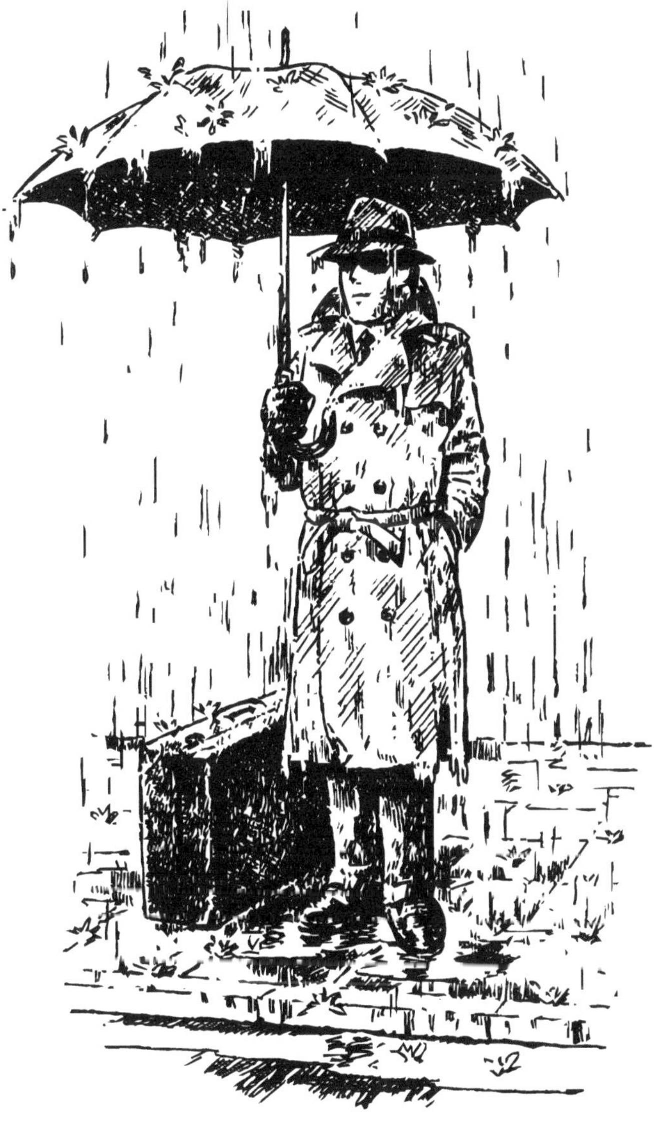

You Sing No More

I hear your call in song no more
As were the rituals of our day
When drums in legions would parade
To usher dancers in their youth
To courtyards in festivity
When harvest time would call again.

We now sing of our broken dreams
With fleeting memories of those days
When sun and moon and stars as one
Would congregate to celebrate
Seasons of peace and bounteousness
When tales of old days were retold
By warriors who had battles won
And bore gay brides on saddled beasts.

These hills and valleys of your land
Has heard no horn or drum in call
To stir their spirit and rejoice
Since freedom by men was proclaimed
While shackled others had remained

In labours and in servitude
To masters of their politics
At the summit of dishonesty.

They bear bad tidings from abroad
In shameless christened liberties
For which our silver and our gold
Were paid to demons of their choice
In the name of democracy
While thirst and hunger that we know
Sank their long fangs into our roots
To decimate our broken race
Whose song will never sound again
As long as they cling on the reins.

You Will Be Borne Again

Just one more moment of decay,
Though bodies among whom you lie
As from dust to dust you return,
Your birth a second time draws near
Is sure as daybreak of each day
For none like you would die in vain.

You will return to us again
Without a tale or memory
Of tombstones or graves where you lie
Before time comes to rise again
And sup the dewdrops of new day
When all the dead will live again
And we as one will dance again
To celebrate eternity.

Although this world stirs in disdain
A throne of comfort you will gain
Among your lovers of those days
When we locked arms in warm embrace
Before you had to go away

And take rest in your hiding place
Beneath the plaque in gold engraved
By sons and daughters who await
Grand seasons as they celebrate
Your second birth on that new day.

About the Author

K I Laibuta EBS depicts our world in prolific works that spice his works of arts in poetry, which took root ahead of his time when he first stepped into the thrilling world of literature and theatre arts. His passion for poetry was inspired by legendary artists who featured in poetry recitals in various theatres in Nairobi. His works attained national acclaim following recitals dedicated to his growing collection of poems, which became a common feature in frequent recitals where he shared the stage in public and private fireside venues with renowned poets who set the pace for generations to come.

K. I. Laibuta's premiere anthology titled *A Race in the Dark* published by Bridgehouse Limited in 2017 elevated his poetry to new heights. His second anthology titled *A Legion of Drums* is yet another milestone in Laibuta's literary exploits building on his contribution in 1986 to Boundless Voices (Heineman Educational Books Nairobi), not to mention numerous pieces featured from time to time in literary magazines and periodicals.

The writer views life with compound eyes that see reality and tell its tales in vivid pictures of the truth depicted in the works of art in his anthologies. As a legal professional and academic, his social commentary in this anthology takes its rightful place in the spoken word by which he leaves nothing untold of private lives in the social-economic and political environments that mute many a tongue.

Milton Keynes UK
Ingram Content Group UK Ltd.
UKHW021116031224
452078UK00011B/895